ALL the INSECTS in the WORLD

David Opie

PETER PAUPER PRESS, INC.
WHITE PLAINS, NEW YORK

Published by Peter Pauper Press, Inc.
202 Mamaroneck Avenue
White Plains, New York 10601 USA

Library of Congress Cataloging-in-Publication Data

Names: Opie, David, author.
Title: All the insects in the world / David Opie, David Opie.
Description: First edition. | White Plains, New York : Peter Pauper Press,
Inc., 2022. | Audience: Ages 3 to 8 | Audience: Grades K-1 | Summary:
"A glimpse into the vast world of insects: their lifespan, how they build
their homes, their color and shape variants, all leading up to their
most amazing attribute--metamorphosis, as seen through the character
of a caterpillar that turns into a butterfly. An informative, non-fiction
children's picture book about insects"-- Provided by publisher.
Identifiers: LCCN 2021054130 | ISBN 9781441335586 (hardcover)
Subjects: LCSH: Insects--Juvenile literature.
Classification: LCC QL467.2 .O65 2022 | DDC 595.7--dc23/eng/20211104
LC record available at https://lccn.loc.gov/2021054130

ISBN 978-1-4413-3558-6
Manufactured for Peter Pauper Press, Inc.
Printed in China

7 6 5 4 3 2 1

Visit us at www.peterpauper.com

Dedicated in memory of my father.

Imagine you shrank to the size of a penny
and walked around outside.
You might see a river of ants,
a swooping dragonfly
scooping up a mosquito,
or a buzzing bumblebee
hovering over a flower,
sipping sweet nectar.
You might even see a twig
staring back at you with its eyes.
And if you look closely,
you'll see the world transform before you
into the busy, bustling domain of insects.

"What would I see if I
looked really closely?"
asked Caterpillar.

Insects have been around
for about 400 million years.
They developed slowly
from the same animals
that gave rise to shrimp, crabs, and lobsters.
Long ago,
when fish pulled themselves out of the oceans,
and onto land,
they found that insects had already been there—
for millions of years!

But what are insects?
They have a hard outer shell
instead of bones on the inside.
Each of their big eyes
contains lots of mini eyes.
They have three main body sections, six legs,
and one pair of antennae.
Insects breathe through rows of holes
along their bodies.
They are born from eggs,
except just a few, like the tsetse fly and tiny aphids.

"Am I an insect?"
asked Caterpillar.

Most insects have wings,
and even the heaviest beetles
can fly!
Insects flew through the air
hundreds of millions of years
before dinosaurs sprouted feathers
and took to the skies.
There are house flies, horseflies, stoneflies, scorpionflies,
dragonflies, fireflies, mayflies, owlflies, and butterflies.

Many insects depend on the sun to stay warm,
and some fly far away
to avoid cold seasons.
Monarch butterflies will travel from Canada to Mexico
to follow the sun's heat.
It can take several generations to complete the journey,
so the butterflies that arrive
are the great-grandchildren of the ones that started.
Some dragonflies and locusts can cross wide oceans,
helped along by gusty breezes.

"Look at them go!"

Bees use their ability to fly far from the hive
to visit many flowers
and feed on their sugary nectar.
Over millions of years, plants developed
colorful, fragrant flowers and sweet nectar
to lure bees and other insects,
who can then spread pollen,
helping the plants multiply.
Insects and flowers developed together,
each depending on the other.

"I wish I could fly and
help the flowers grow!"

11

Insects are round, flat, wide, skinny,
or any shape in between.
Beetles can be oval and massive,
and sprout long horns
or have huge jaws,
while some mantises and katydids
look just like leaves.
One of the smallest insects is the fairy wasp,
not much bigger
than the comma in this sentence.
A white witch moth's wings
can spread wider than a sparrow's.
One of the heaviest insects
is the giant weta,
found in New Zealand.
The giant weta can weigh
more than a house mouse.
And the longest insects
look like tree branches.

"Are you sure that's
not just a leaf?"

Many insects are colored gray, brown, and green,
to disappear into their surroundings.
Yet other insects
will flash warnings
with their bright colors and patterns:
"Stay away from me, I'm poisonous," they say.
And some beetles shimmer and shine,
like jewels with legs.

Scientists have named
about a million species of insects,
but there are probably millions more,
waiting to be identified.
The most common type, or "order," of insect is the beetle.
There are over 350,000 known beetle species.

You can tell a beetle
by its hard outer wing case.
The fastest runner in the insect world
is the Australian tiger beetle,
which scampers so fast,
its eyesight blurs
when sprinting at top speed.

"Hey, slow down!
I'm trying to
count you all!"

Some insects are great builders.
Paper wasps construct homes
from chewed scraps of plant fibers.
Termites can build towering mounds
out of soil and their own droppings.
Ants build huge underground cities
to house millions in their colonies.
Their tunneling helps renew the soil,
spreading nutrients and fertilizing it.

Bagworm caterpillars build little houses,
out of whatever material they have around them.
Some look like tiny log cabins,
which they carry around on their backs
like a hermit crab carries its shell.
Caddisfly larvae
will spin a silk case for themselves
and attach little scraps to it,
protecting them while they grow
in freshwater streams and ponds.

"What can I build?"
asked Caterpillar.

19

Insects have spread
to just about every place on the planet,
including freshwater streams and lakes,
although very few insects can survive in saltwater.
Water striders use the tiny hairs on their long legs
to stay afloat
as they skim across ponds.

Water boatmen beetles have back legs shaped like oars
that they can paddle underwater.
Great diving beetles can swim underwater, too.
They trap air from the surface
and hold it underneath their wings
while they dive
and snag little fish and tadpoles
for an underwater meal.

"Insects can do so
many great things!
What can I do?"

Insects change in several ways
throughout their lives.
Young insects outgrow their hard outer shell,
and shed it in a process known as "molting."
When insects molt, they bust out of their old shell
and wait for their soft new skin
to dry and harden into fresh protective armor.
This process can regrow damaged legs and other parts.
Insects can molt many times during their lives.
But that's not even their biggest transformation . . .

. . . Just about all insects come from eggs,
and then live for a while in their baby stage, called a larva.
The larva undergoes a dramatic change
called "metamorphosis,"
in which it becomes an adult.

23

One of the biggest transformations of all
occurs in butterflies and moths.
The process starts for the monarch butterfly
with a tiny egg laid on the underside of a milkweed leaf.
The egg hatches into a caterpillar:
a soft, worm-like animal
with small eyes
and no wings.

The caterpillar eats and eats,
and molts several times as it grows.

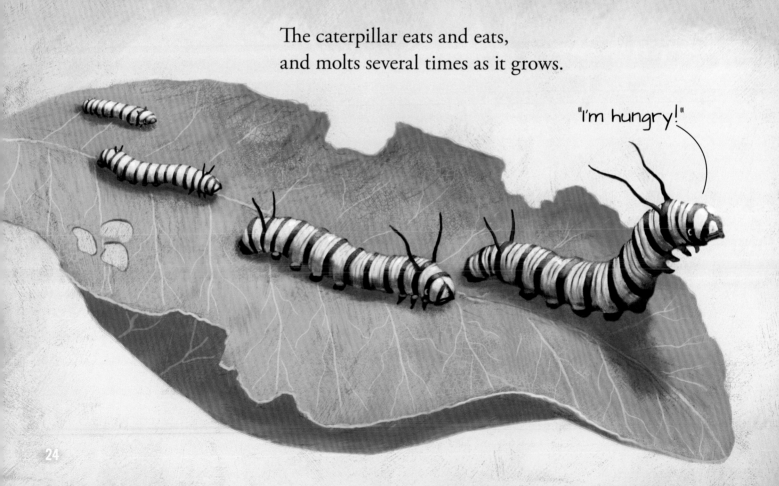

The caterpillar forms a protective chrysalis,
and inside that case,
something magical starts to happen.
Something that will completely change the caterpillar forever.
Look closely.

"Now
I
can..."

"...FLY!"

Said Butterfly,
who was no longer Caterpillar.

A Note from the Author

While doing research for this book, I shared insect drawings and studies on social media and told people what I was working on. For many of them, a look of disgust would wash over their face. "Ew, I don't really like bugs," they'd say. I got that reaction a lot.

I already mentioned in this book that insects are vital to plants because they spread pollen, which helps plants reproduce, and that insect tunneling enriches the soil. They also help break down animal droppings, rotting trees, and dead animals, which returns nutrients to the ecosystem. In addition, insects are an important link in the food chain. Without them, many birds, reptiles, and mammals would starve.

Sure, some insects, like flies and mosquitoes, can spread diseases to us humans, but the overwhelming majority of them don't. As the Harvard entomologist and author E. O. Wilson noted, if humans were to disappear from the face of the Earth, the natural world would keep on thriving. But if insects were to become extinct, "the terrestrial environment would collapse into chaos." That's right: A healthy insect population is critical to the health of our planet.

Insects are amazing animals by just about any measure. Let's review a few facts: Insects have been

around for about 400 million years. Their ancestors were the first to colonize land, and insects were the first animals to take flight. Entomologists estimate that there are more than 200 million individual insects living today for every human being who's currently alive. The online database "Catalogue of Life" lists about 953,000 identified species of insects (and entomologists agree that there are more unknown insect species than species that have been identified). Contrast that with about 34,000 known species of fish, about 6,000 mammal species, and about 10,000 bird species, and you'll understand how vast the insect class really is.

In spite of those impressively big numbers, evidence suggests that insect populations are in major decline because of things like global climate change, destruction of their natural habitats, and the use of pesticides and fertilizers. We humans share the planet with these animals. They need our help—and we need theirs. To find out more about insect (and other invertebrate) conservation, including individual things that you can do, please visit the Xerces Society at www.xerces.org.

I discovered that the more I learned about insects, the more fascinating they became. I hope the same happens for you!

(Top) Buff-tailed bumblebee. (Bottom, from left) Dogbane beetle, Stag beetle

About Monarch Butterflies

The colorful, high-contrast markings on the wings of monarch butterflies warn insect-eating birds and other predators that monarchs don't taste good, and even contain some toxins from eating the milkweed plant. The monarch butterflies are able to store the toxin from the plant that they fed on as caterpillars, without being affected by the poison. This warning coloration, called "aposematic" marking, protects the monarch butterflies as well as the potential predators.

Monarch butterflies are known for migrating great distances. The eastern monarchs fly from the Great Plains (USA), the American Northeast, and Canada to spend the winter in the much warmer climate of Central Mexico. The western population spends the breeding season in a variety of spots west of the Rocky Mountains and winters in the southern part of California. There are also populations in Portugal, Spain, Hawaii, Australia, and New Zealand. The overall population of monarchs has plummeted since the 1980s, which is why we have to do everything we can to help protect the environment so that caterpillars (like our friend in this book!) can grow and flourish into beautiful butterflies.

Glossary

aphid: A small insect that often lives in large groups and feeds on plant juices.

chrysalis: The hard outer case that protects an insect during metamorphosis.

colony: A community of insects.

entomologist: A scientist who studies insects.

larva: The early stage of an insect after hatching from an egg and before becoming an adult.

mammals: A group of warm-blooded animals that generally have hair or fur, are supported by an internal skeleton, give birth to live young (as opposed to laying eggs), breathe air with lungs, and feed their young on milk produced by females. Examples are mice, dogs, cows, whales, and humans.

metamorphosis: The process an insect goes through in changing from a larva into an adult.

molting: The process an insect goes through when it sheds its outer covering and replaces it with a new one in order to grow.

reptile: A class of animal that is usually covered in scales or bony plates, cannot keep a constant body temperature, and is born from eggs. Examples are lizards, snakes, alligators, and turtles.

skeleton: The internal parts of some animals (like mammals, reptiles, and fish) that support the body and are usually made of bone or cartilage.

Identification

Cover

1. Monarch butterfly
2. June beetle
3. Paper wasps (in background)
4. Picasso bug
5. Blue orchard bee
6. Unarmed stick insect
7. Ulysses butterfly
8. Polyphemus moth
9. Common eastern bumblebee
10. Leaf insect
11. Thorn bug

12. Tiger swallowtail butterfly
13. Hummingbird hawk-moth
14. Green looper caterpillar
15. Modest katydid
16. Green darner dragonfly
17. Buff-tailed bumblebee
18. Monarch butterfly
19. Housefly
20. Painted lady butterfly
21. Blue-tailed damselfly
22. Giraffe weevil

23. Four-banded longhorn beetle
24. Periodical cicada
25. Golden tortoise beetle
26. Jewel beetle
27. European mantis
28. Convergent ladybug
29. European honeybee
30. Rosy maple moth
31. Common eastern firefly
32. Rhinoceros beetle
33. Striped shield bug

34. Field cricket
35. Scarlet lily beetle
36. Acorn weevil
37. Asian lady beetle larva
38. American grasshopper
39. Common red soldier beetle
40. Colorado potato beetle
41. Green rose chafer beetle
42. Carpenter ant
43. Monarch caterpillar

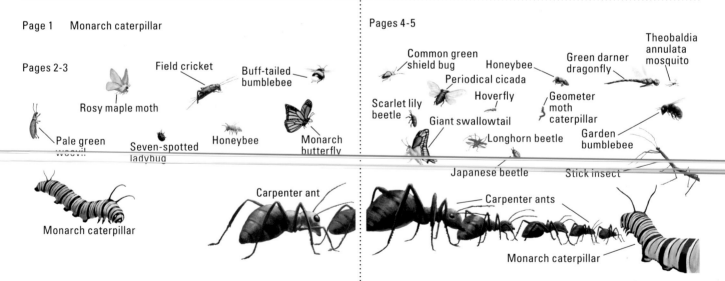

Page 1   Monarch caterpillar

Pages 2-3

Rosy maple moth

Field cricket

Buff-tailed bumblebee

Pale green weevil

Seven-spotted ladybug

Honeybee

Monarch butterfly

Monarch caterpillar

Carpenter ant

Pages 4-5

Common green shield bug

Honeybee

Green darner dragonfly

Theobaldia annulata mosquito

Periodical cicada

Scarlet lily beetle

Hoverfly

Geometer moth caterpillar

Giant swallowtail

Longhorn beetle

Garden bumblebee

Japanese beetle

Stick insect

Carpenter ants

Monarch caterpillar

Page 6   (From top) Red milkweed beetle, Tiger swallowtail butterfly, Yellowjacket, Housefly

Page 7   (From top) Periodical cicada, American grasshopper, Monarch caterpillar

Insects are not necessarily to scale.

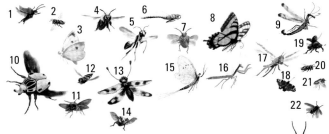

1. Scarlet lily beetle
2. Honeybee
3. Cabbage white butterfly
4. Common eastern bumblebee
5. Black and yellow mud dauber wasp
6. Green darner dragonfly
7. Green shield bug
8. Eastern tiger swallowtail butterfly
9. Scorpion fly
10. Goliath beetle
11. Elephant hawk-moth
12. Hoverfly

13. Owlfly
14. Japanese beetle
15. Mayfly
16. European mantis
17. Desert locust
18. Peacock butterfly
19. Scarab beetle
20. Honeybee
21. Housefly
22. Firefly
23. Monarch caterpillar

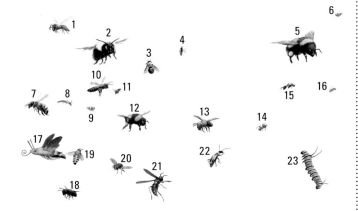

1. Green sweat bee
2. Common eastern bumblebee
3. Eastern carpenter bee
4. Sweat bee
5. Yellow-banded bumblebee
6. Early bumblebee
7. Honeybee
8. Furrow bee
9. Early bumblebee
10. Leafcutter bee
11. Honeybee
12. White-tailed bumblebee

13. Green sweat bee
14. Bumblebee
15. Honeybee
16. Honeybee
17. Hummingbird hawk-moth
18. Blue orchard bee
19. Honeybee
20. Housefly
21. Red paper wasp
22. Goldenrod soldier beetle
23. Monarch caterpillar

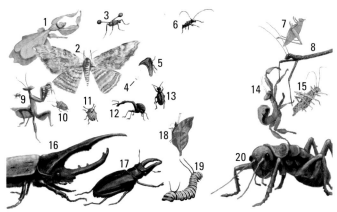

1. Leaf insect
2. White witch moth
3. Stalk-eyed fly
4. Fairy wasp
5. Thorn bug
6. Pine sawyer beetle
7. Modest katydid
8. Stick insect
9. Orchid mantis
10. Green shield bug

11. Colorado potato beetle
12. Giraffe weevil
13. Scarlet lily beetle
14. Giant prickly stick insect
15. Lichen katydid
16. Hercules beetle
17. Stag beetle
18. Dead leaf butterfly
19. Monarch caterpillar
20. Giant weta

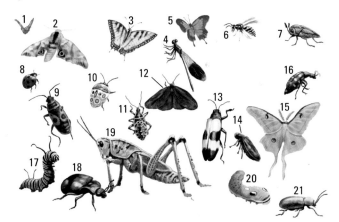

1. Monarch butterfly
2. Eyed hawk-moth
3. Tiger swallowtail
4. River jewelwing
5. Ulysses butterfly
6. Yellowjacket
7. Jewel beetle
8. Seven-spotted ladybug
9. Red soldier bug
10. Picasso bug
11. Mesquite bug nymph

12. Cinnabar moth
13. Banded jewel beetle
14. Red and black froghopper
15. Luna moth
16. Blister beetle
17. Monarch caterpillar
18. Handsome fungus beetle
19. Eastern lubber grasshopper
20. Spicebush swallowtail caterpillar
21. Dogbane beetle

Insects are not necessarily to scale.

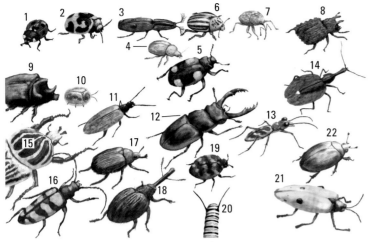
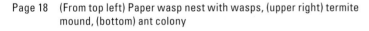
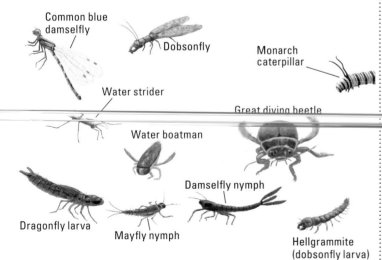

1. Seven-spotted ladybug
2. Milkweed leaf beetle
3. Madagascar click beetle
4. Tansy beetle
5. Yellow-spotted handsome fungus beetle
6. Colorado potato beetle
7. Acorn weevil
8. Forked fungus beetle
9. Rhinoceros beetle
10. Golden tortoise beetle
11. Darkling beetle

12. Stag beetle
13. Tiger beetle
14. Violin beetle
15. Goliath beetle
16. Banded longhorn beetle
17. Japanese beetle
18. Rose weevil
19. Carpet beetle
20. Monarch caterpillar
21. Leaf beetle
22. Jewel scarab

Page 18   (From top left) Paper wasp nest with wasps, (upper right) termite mound, (bottom) ant colony

Page 19   (From top) Paper wasps in background, Bagworm moth caterpillar cocoons made of little pieces of wood (left) and pine needles (right), Monarch caterpillar, Caddisfly larva (at bottom)

Pages 20-21

Common blue damselfly

Dobsonfly

Monarch caterpillar

Water strider

Great diving beetle

Water boatman

Damselfly nymph

Dragonfly larva

Mayfly nymph

Hellgrammite (dobsonfly larva)

Insects are not necessarily to scale.

Page 22

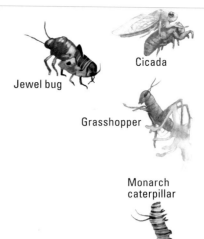

Jewel bug

Cicada

Grasshopper

Monarch caterpillar

Page 23

Antlion

Stag beetle

Ladybug

Honeybee

Green darner dragonfly

Page 24   (Top) The small dot on the bottom of the leaf is a monarch butterfly egg. The caterpillar on the top of the leaf is the first stage (or instar) of the monarch caterpillar.
(Bottom) Different stages of a monarch caterpillar.

Page 25   (Left to right) Monarch caterpillar (or larva), spinning a cocoon, pupa (or chrysalis), monarch butterfly emerging from pupal stage

Pages 26-27 Monarch butterfly